HEAVEN SPEAKS TO THOSE CONSIDERING SUICIDE

Direction for Our Times
As given to Anne, a lay apostle

Heaven Speaks to Those Considering Suicide

Direction for Our Times
As given to Anne, a lay apostle

ISBN: 978-1-933684-28-4

© Copyright 2007-2012 Direction for Our Times. All rights reserved. No part of this book may be used or reproduced in any manner whatsoever without written permission.

Publisher:
Direction for Our Times
9000 West 81st Street
Justice, IL 60458
708-496-9300
contactus@directionforourtimes.org

www.directionforourtimes.org

Manufactured in the United States of America

Direction for Our Times is a 501(c)(3) tax-exempt organization.

Direction for Our Times wishes to manifest its complete obedience and submission of mind and heart to the final and definitive judgment of the Magisterium of the Catholic Church and the local Ordinary regarding the supernatural character of the messages received by Anne, a lay apostle.

In this spirit, the messages of Anne, a lay apostle, have been submitted to her bishop, Most Reverend Leo O'Reilly, Bishop of Kilmore, Ireland, and to the Vatican Congregation for the Doctrine of the Faith for formal examination. In the meantime Bishop O'Reilly has given permission for their publication.

Table of Contents

November 29, 2006
  Jesus 1

November 30, 2006
  St. Margaret Mary Alacoque 4
  St. Margaret Mary Alacoque 7

December 1, 2006
  St. Margaret Mary Alacoque 10
  St. Margaret Mary Alacoque 12
  Blessed Mother 14

November 29, 2006
Jesus

I have many things to say to those who are considering this act of self-harm. I love you. I see your pain. I understand that you long for relief from your anguish. Please, bring your anguish to Me. I can help you. You are so valuable to the Kingdom and I need you to help bring Me to others.

"How?" you say, in your great interior grief. "How could I possibly be helpful to Jesus and to others?"

I will tell you. Your pain is the pain of many in the world today. Many souls feel your grief, your hopelessness. Many carry heavy crosses of illness and addiction, loneliness and hopelessness, rejection and anxiety. Many of My children look into their future and see only more grief and pain and this takes their courage from them. Dearest friend, you must not do this. Do not look into tomorrow and expect today's pain to be repeated. You are not certain of such an occurrence. You cannot be certain because I, God, could change your life during this day, today. You must remain in this day, in the present, because I have given you adequate grace to deal with your cross. It is only when you look into the future and think that your Jesus will send you no relief that you find life unmanageable. Understand this. Your life is only unmanageable if you put Me out of it. If you let Me into your heart, into your life, I will make it not only manageable, but joyful.

You are skeptical. You cannot believe in a future with joy because the present holds such pain. I understand this, just as I understand everything about you. You may not know Me well so I will tell you something about Myself that may help you to decide that trusting Me is a good decision.

I have never been known to break a promise. Never. Today, I have a promise for you.

If you ask Me to help you, I will help you. Ask Me, My beloved one. You are important to this Kingdom and I have a plan for you. I need you. I need you to serve in a way that you do not and cannot understand today, in your great hopelessness. I will reveal the plan but you will have to be courageous and allow Me to move you from this place of despair to a place of hope in your heart. I will do so. I will move you along, away from your sadness. You must trust Me just a little bit and give me just a little bit of time. Even now, as you read these words, hope is stirring within you. This hope is from Me and it is the smallest indication of what I will bring to you. I am giving you courage. I am giving you hope. Rest with Me.

Say this, "I will rest myself against Jesus and wait for Him to send relief."

I will send relief. Do not be afraid. I am with you now and I will never leave you.

November 30, 2006
St. Margaret Mary Alacoque

Dear little soul, you are in pain. Your anguish feels deep, I know. Often, the most difficult part of suffering anguish is the perception that nobody understands the depth of your pain. One can feel very alone in such pain and when one seeks out consolation from others, one is often terribly disappointed. Please listen to me. I am your sister in Christ. I experienced great anguishes while I was on earth so I am rejoicing that God allows me to help you. When you go to another seeking comfort and you find yourself in worse shape, feeling even more misunderstood and alone, you must come to me. Say, "Margaret, I need help. I need help now."

I, Margaret, will go directly to the throne of God and I will remain there until you receive the comfort and courage you require. My friend, it is important that you know that you are not suffering alone. Jesus sees your suffering. He feels it with you and His Sacred Heart is moved to the most passionate desire to assist you. You must allow our Jesus to help you. When you make this emergency prayer to me, Margaret, you are really saying that you are willing to let heaven help you. How heaven rushes in at this time! You will know that I have heard you because you will feel a change. It may be just a whisper of a change, just a little shifting. It will be noticeable to you as a feeling of calm in your spirit. When you feel this little feeling of calm, you will know that you have been heard, that help is on the way and that you are not alone in your suffering. You have my promise that heaven will surround you until the frightening feelings pass.

I want to say something else. It is common for a person on earth to have thoughts that are not from God. Everyone on earth struggles with this at some time. We could say, actually, that everyone on earth struggles with this each day in terms of temptations. The battle is not finished until you die in your body and come to God's Kingdom. Given this, the constant need for struggle, you must view your thoughts of suicide as temptations. Do not be alarmed by these thoughts in that simply having these thoughts does not mean there is any reason to act on these thoughts. Do you understand? Do not be afraid. We, the saints in heaven, all had bad thoughts and temptations during our time on earth and we all at times failed to fight off temptations. The temptation to commit suicide is one where you must fight hard, with everything you have because of the nature of the consequence. If you take your life, you will not be able to go back and say, "Jesus, I want to do better and serve You now." You take away any second chances for yourself to convert to Jesus and try again. Dear friends, this is wrong for you. It is not the answer you are seeking.

Jesus needs you to stay in the world until it is the right time for you to come home. This is God's plan and it is always best to follow God's plan. The last day of your life is determined by God. You must not think that the answer to great pain is suicide. This act of self-harm is always a mistake. Always.

St. Margaret Mary Alacoque

My friend, you have been hurt. I see that. I understand that you are carrying wounds that cause you to ache. You may not even understand the source of your pain and your wounds. You know that you are not perfect and that you make mistakes. Jesus accepts this about you and loves you most tenderly regardless of your mistakes. I want you to consider that others also make mistakes. Others fail in love and in kindness. Others are imperfect as we were all imperfect on earth. The mistakes made by others can cause us the greatest pain. We can carry wounds with us without even being aware that we are doing so. These wounds then spread to other areas of our hearts and result in a general state of pain that is hard to come back from.

Jesus suffered terribly on earth. He also carried wounds. Jesus, in His most Sacred Heart, understands exactly how you came to be in such pain. He knows more about the source of your pain and hopelessness than you do. My beloved friend, I beg you now to turn to Jesus. He will heal you from wounds you do not even know you are carrying. You have felt loss in your life and there is emptiness. Jesus will fill you up again and restore you to a state of hope and joy that will flow out from you to others. I am telling you that your great pain will recede. When your great pain recedes and joy takes its place, you will be so kind to others because you will understand how they are hurting. You will look at another in anguish and your heart will be moved to the greatest pity for him. You will say, "I remember feeling that badly." Only one who has suffered such anguish can really understand it. Would you agree? Do you remember a time when you spoke to someone about something that he had also experienced and you felt understood? It will be this way with your great pain, also, and someone who feels hopeless will gain hope from you. If you take your life, you will not be around to help this person in the future.

I want you to know that Jesus, in His most Sacred Heart, feels your pain. Jesus suffered so that we could be forgiven. The fact that Jesus suffered willingly does not in any way take away from the fact that Jesus suffered terribly. Perhaps, my friend, you can look up to Jesus and tell Him that you, in your suffering, understand something about His suffering. If you do this, all of heaven will rejoice because you will be on your way to becoming a saint. Believe this, my friend, because it is truth. Many will share with Jesus in His joy. Many will even respect His cross. But few are there on earth who will carry the cross and turn their eyes to the Lord in love during their suffering, which is what Jesus did. Do this, beloved one, and heaven will lighten your cross and remove this pain more quickly than you expect.

December 1, 2006
St. Margaret Mary Alacoque

I feel such compassion for you, my friend. When you are carrying a heavy cross, it is difficult to see that it will end. Sometimes, you do not believe it will ever end. In terms of human power, maybe it is even impossible that your cross will end. But nothing is impossible for heaven. In heaven, you see, we live with miracles happening all around us. When you come to heaven you will understand what I mean. If your situation requires a miracle from heaven, you should ask for one. Miracles are not impossible when you keep company with saints. Saints, indeed, are all about obtaining miracles from God. God gives us these things, these miracles, because we suffered with Him while we were on earth. You will be a saint if you suffer with Jesus. And then you will be able to obtain powerful graces, also. You will say, "God, please help this person." God will do so when He sees that you are making the smallest effort to accept your suffering with Jesus. You have influence in your suffering. You have intercessory power, which means that if you ask for graces for another, God will grant them.

This may be difficult for you to accept because you feel so sad or angry but I will use my influence to obtain graces for you to help you to understand. You will see that your suffering, your pain, is being used by heaven to help others. It will pass, my friend. You will feel better. I make this promise to you in the presence of Jesus Christ. He will keep this promise for us.

St. Margaret Mary Alacoque

I am going to give you some advice. I am one who suffered great anguish on earth, as I said, so I am a good one to help you. Remain very calm during this time of upset. Do not panic. Do not act in haste. Let us, your heavenly friends, calm your spirit. If you deal with your pain in quiet, with an attitude of calm, you will be less likely to make bad decisions that create even more pain. It is best, indeed, if you can delay important decisions until you feel better. Be wise about your suffering and allow yourself to be quiet. This is not a bad thing. Spending time in silence, reflecting, will not harm you. While you are remaining in quiet, ask Jesus constantly for help. Ask Him to remove your pain as soon as possible, and ask Him to help others who are suffering this pain. You are joined to heaven, remember, so there are many of us in heaven who understand that you are suffering and seek to help you. You are not alone. We will never abandon you in your anguish. Ask heaven to send you calming graces and heaven will do so. Remember that you are important and that we love you very much. Your mistakes do not affect our love for you because we made mistakes, too. Heaven is filled with saints who were great sinners on earth. We repented and God forgave us. Be at peace about your mistakes because the experience you gain from your mistakes helps you later. Do you understand? God has a plan for you. Taking your life is not part of that plan. You are surrounded by saints and you are surrounded by angels. You belong to our family and you will have all that you need.

Blessed Mother

My dear little child, how heavy is your heart. I see that you are suffering and feeling alone. Dear beloved one, you are not alone now and you will never be alone. Even as you read these words, heaven surrounds you. The angels pray constantly for your recovery, for a return to joy for you. You must believe that I tell you the truth today. I am Mary, your mother, and I can only seek what is good for you. I will seek what is good for you right now, before the throne of God, and ask the Father to send you heavenly gifts of courage and calm. You will move through this day that is already passing into the past and tomorrow will be better. Each day will move you closer to recovery. Do not think for a moment that God will leave you with pain that is unmanageable. God will not do this. Ask for help and you will receive it. I am here, with you now, and I will make sure that you receive all that you need to move past this period of anguish. Heaven does not will this for you. Heaven wills hope for you. Heavenly graces filled with hope flow into your soul now. Rest in God's grace and I will secure all that is necessary for you. I am your mother. I love you completely. I will help you. May I ask you to help me with something? I ask that you turn away from anything that is causing you this pain. Walk away from habits that bring darkness into your little soul. I will give you the light to understand what is creating such pain. You will not be left confused. Your cross will be lightened. You have my assurance of this. Be at peace today because, truly, heaven hears your prayer and moves to answer your prayer. You will see heaven helping you in many ways, my beloved child. You are not alone.

Lay Apostles of Jesus Christ the Returning King

We seek to be united to Jesus in our daily work, and through our vocations, in order to obtain graces for the conversion of sinners. We pledge our allegiance to God the Father. Through our cooperation with the Holy Spirit, we will allow Jesus to flow through us into the world, bringing His light. We do this in union with Mary, our Blessed Mother, with the Communion of Saints, with all of God's holy angels, and with our fellow lay apostles in the world.

As lay apostles of Jesus Christ the Returning King, we agree to adopt the following spiritual practices, as best we can.

1. Allegiance Prayer, along with the Morning Offering and a brief prayer for the Holy Father.

2. One hour of Eucharistic Adoration each week.

3. Participation in a monthly lay apostle prayer group, which includes the Luminous Mysteries of the Holy Rosary, and the reading of the Monthly Message.

4. Monthly Confession.

5. Further, we will follow the example of Jesus Christ as set out in Holy Scripture, treating all others with His patience and kindness.

Promise from Jesus to His Lay Apostles:

May 12, 2005

Your message to souls remains constant. Welcome each soul to the rescue mission. You may assure each lay apostle that just as they concern themselves with My interests, I will concern Myself with theirs. They will be placed in My Sacred Heart and I will defend and protect them. I will also pursue complete conversion of each of their loved ones. So you see, the souls who serve in this rescue mission as My beloved lay apostles will know peace. The world cannot make this promise, as only heaven can bestow peace on a soul. This is truly heaven's mission and I call every one of heaven's children to assist Me. You will be well rewarded, My dear ones.

Allegiance Prayer

Dear God in heaven, I pledge my allegiance to You. I give You my life, my work, and my heart. In turn, give me the grace of obeying Your every direction to the fullest possible extent. Amen.

Morning Offering

O Jesus, through the Immaculate Heart of Mary, I offer You the prayers, works, joys, and sufferings of this day, for all the intentions of Your Sacred Heart, in union with the Holy Sacrifice of the Mass throughout the world, in reparation for my sins, and for the intentions of the Holy Father. Amen.

Five Luminous Mysteries:

1. The Baptism of Jesus
2. The Wedding at Cana
3. The Proclamation of the Kingdom of God
4. The Transfiguration
5. The Institution of the Eucharist

The Volumes

*Direction for Our Times
as given to Anne, a lay apostle*

Volume One:	***Thoughts on Spirituality***
Volume Two:	***Conversations with the Eucharistic Heart of Jesus***
Volume Three:	***God the Father Speaks to His Children*** ***The Blessed Mother Speaks to Her Bishops and Priests***
Volume Four:	***Jesus the King*** ***Heaven Speaks to Priests*** ***Jesus Speaks to Sinners***
Volume Six:	***Heaven Speaks to Families***
Volume Seven:	***Greetings from Heaven***
Volume Nine:	***Angels***
Volume Ten:	***Jesus Speaks to His Apostles***

Volumes Five and Eight will be printed at a later date.

The Volumes are now available in PDF format for free download and printing from our website:
www.directionforourtimes.org.
We encourage everyone to print and distribute them.

The Volumes are also available at your local bookstore.

The "Heaven Speaks" Booklets

*Direction for Our Times
as given to Anne, a lay apostle*

The following booklets are available individually from Direction for Our Times:

Heaven Speaks About Abortion
Heaven Speaks About Addictions
Heaven Speaks to Victims of Clerical Abuse
Heaven Speaks to Consecrated Souls
Heaven Speaks About Depression
Heaven Speaks About Divorce
Heaven Speaks to Prisoners
Heaven Speaks to Soldiers
Heaven Speaks About Stress
Heaven Speaks to Young Adults

Heaven Speaks to Those Away from the Church
Heaven Speaks to Those Considering Suicide
Heaven Speaks to Those Who Do Not Know Jesus
Heaven Speaks to Those Who Are Dying
Heaven Speaks to Those Who Experience Tragedy
Heaven Speaks to Those Who Fear Purgatory
Heaven Speaks to Those Who Have Rejected God
Heaven Speaks to Those Who Struggle to Forgive
Heaven Speaks to Those Who Suffer from Financial Need
Heaven Speaks to Parents Who Worry About Their Children's Salvation

All twenty of the "Heaven Speaks" booklets are now available in PDF format for free download and printing from our website www.directionforourtimes.org. We encourage everyone to print and distribute these booklets.

This book is part of a non-profit mission.
Our Lord has requested that we
spread these words internationally.

Please help us.

If you would like to participate,
please contact us at:

Direction for Our Times
9000 West 81st Street
Justice, Illinois 60458

708-496-9300
contactus@directionforourtimes.org
www.directionforourtimes.org

Direction for Our Times Ireland
The Hague Building
Cullies
Cavan
County Cavan
Ireland

Phone: 353-(0)49-437-3040
Email: contactus@dfot.ie

Jesus gives Anne a message for the
world on the first day of each month.
To receive the monthly messages
you may access our website at
www.directionforourtimes.org
or call us at 708-496-9300
to be placed on our mailing list.